Ancestral Logic
&
CaribbeanBlues

AncestralLogic
&
CaribbeanBlues

by

Kofi Anyidoho

Africa World Press, Inc.
P.O. Box 1892
Trenton, New Jersey 08607

Africa World Press
P.O. Box 1892
Trenton NJ 08607

Copyright © Kofi Anyidoho, 1993

First Printing, Africa World Press, 1993

Cover and Book Design by Jonathan Gullery

Cover photo by Susanne Gott

Library of Congress Catalog Card Number: 91-75601

ISBN: 0-86543-264-3 Cloth
        0-86543-265-1 Paper

to the memory
of
Sara Lee
& for
Robert Lee

for
the love, the bravery
of their choice.

&
to
Akosua & Akofa

for
sharing the American solitude

&
to
Akua, Cudjoe, Hannah & Kate
for
walking in balance back at home.

Acknowledgements

Some of these poems have previously appeared in various publications: "Lolita Jones" and "Santrofi" in *Uhuru* magazine; "DesertStorm" in *West Africa* magazine; "Nostalgia", "AirZimbabwe" and "Bayonets" in *African Commentary*. The three transitional poems—"EarthChild", "The Song of a Twin Brother" and "Fertility-Game" appear in my earlier collections *Earthchild with Brain Surgery* (1985) and *A Harvest of Our Dreams* (1984; 1985).

***

This collection was finalized during my term at the Africana Studies & Research Center, Cornell University, as a 1990-91 Visiting Faculty Fellow of the Program in African Cultural Studies sponsored by the Rockefeller Foundation. My gratitude goes to the Africana Center and the sponsors; to the faculty and staff for their support: Anne Adams, Beverly Blacksher, Bill Branch, Bill Cross, Locksley Edmondson, Girma Kebbede, Abdul Nanji, Don Ohadike, James Turner, Marvin Williams. To Tom Weissinger, the Librarian, and his Assistant Eric Acree for being there with all the books we need for sorting out our brains. For their concern and their handling of the administrative burden of my stay, I am greatly indebted to Bob Harris, Director, and his staff: Daisy Rowe, Sheila Towner, and Carolyn Wells. For the many hours of sharing our work & dreams and forever worrying over our ancestral past and our future heritage, I cannot be thankful enough to Femi Taiwo [who shared the fellowship year and an office with me], to Dotsevi Sogah and to Biodun Jeyifo, and of course to Christie & Kofi Agawu whose house was my other home.

TABLE OF CONTENTS

IntroBlues

There is a journey we all must make into our past in order to come to terms with our future. In the last decade or so I have journeyed into various spaces of the world. And everywhere I go I must confront dimensions of myself I did not know were there. I discover new purposes I did not know I could have made my own. There is something of my-story carved into every tombstone in all the graveyards of the world, something of my history enshrined in every monument and in every anthem ever erected in honour of the spirit of endurance. Back home in Africa, we perform our resurrection dance in the company of hyenas pretending to be royal ancestors. They tell us our salvation lies in a repudiation of our history of pain and of endless fragmentation. But I journeyed to Giessen in the heart of AryanEarth and there in the company of Mervyn Morris and Carolyn Cooper, of Caryl Phillips and Joan Riley and Marlene Philip, of Chinjerai Hove and Anthony Nazombe, together, we sorted out our differences and found an ancestral unison in the midst of provocative distractions.

The official programme defined our being together in terms of the common alien tongue grafted into our creative souls by an extinguished colonial empire; we were representative contributors to *The New Literatures in English*, an alternative term to what used to be called *Commonwealth Literature* until the CommonWealth Ideal could no longer be reconciled to the arrogant opulence of the few in full view of the despair of the many.

As a people whose life is eternally defined by the paradox of Africa's historical consciousness, we gathered in Giessen on the premise of our shared inheritance of English as an uncommon language of creativity, but we soon discovered that there were shared concerns and shared ways of articulating our concerns in a manner our common linguistic legacy could neither explain nor contain. Sometimes even the owners of this proud legacy would stand puzzled as we wandered through history and memory, seeking lost landmarks, often proceeding with an intuitive logic marked by a geography of scars and by the inescapable "living wound under a patchwork of scars." We would shock ourselves with unsuspected ecstacy as we stumbled upon hidden paths that point in directions of a future unmarked by scars, a future relieved of the eternal burden of a generation without elders and often withhout heirs:

> In the half-life, half-light of alien tongues,
> In the uncanny fluency of the other's language
> We relive the past in rituals of revival,
> Unravelling memories in slow time; gathering the present.
> (Abena Busia, "Migrations").

Ours is the IntroBlues, the forever journey into SoulTime. It is the quest for a future alive with the energy of recovered vision, a future released from the trauma of a cyclonic past and from the myopia of a stampeded present. It cannot mustnot be that the rest of the world, with our own connivance, came upon us, picked us up, used us to clean up her mess, then dropped us off into trash, and moved on into a new era of celebrative arrogance, somehow hopeful that we will forever remain in the shadows of our own doubts. The wounds must be sought out and washed clean with the iodine of pain. The trauma of death must be transformed into the drama of life, the destabilized soul purged of the heavy burden of permanent sorrow and of recurring seizures of rage.

The quest for recovered vision begins as a confrontation with the grey mythology of little minds forever lost in the blinding flash of the electrocuted dream. Always we must recall the fate of those who fought to the death of the last warrior, to the death of the final hope.

They say Christoph Colomb rode the waves and landed in

a dream. They say he discovered a people as organized as the beehive. They say he claimed the honey for the unquenchable thirst of His Majesty the King of Spain. He set the hive ablaze to quench his own greed for fame. Four Hundred and Ninety-Eight Years later, I journey from Africa into Santo Domingo and find an island still standing in the sea of blood, lying deep in the path of hurricanes. In 1992 an uncaring world celebrates Christoph Colomb in full view of those who still pay the price of other people's ecstasy. The Taino-Arawaks, they who discovered Christoph Colomb and died upon their inalienable love for their Earth, are now mere momentos packaged into flimsy toys for tourist collectors of little treasures. And yet the troubled presence of their absence casts long shadows upon the marbled whorehouses that line the sandy beaches of this stolen legacy.

Adios Domingo. And yet must I take with me memories of those who put some meaning to my nightmare. Pedro Muamba Tujibikile, the brother Catholic priest from Zaire, now doing missionary work among the peasants of Republica Dominicana. He it was who wrote and spoke of *La Resistencia cultural del negro en America Latina: Logica ancestral y celebracion de la vida* . Perhaps one day I may learn of how this ancestral logic works. How do our people, trapped as they are in this 20th century sugar plantaion colony, how do they celebrate life in a land where all people of African decent are mislabeled *Indios* , and you could not call yourself a Negro no matter how far you insist on journeying into SoulTime. Adios Domingo.

My journey from Santo Domingo into Havana was like making a connection between two lifetimes separated by a final death of the soul. Many telexes back and forth, and against the best judgment of travel agents who could not find Havana listed in their most comprehensive travel guides, I finally sit on Cubana Air and hop the brief distance into another life, across the Bay of Pigs. And Havana was quiet and thoughtful of the sudden death of old friendships, as the Eastern Block collapsed from weight of communal dreams pressed too hard against the push of freedomways. And Havana's solitude is also Havana's fortitude. *Socialismo o Muerte* !

And so I come to the U.S. of A., and in the year of Crisis in the Gulf. You could feel the gentle stirrings of the winds, then the rising burst of self-righteous anger, the sudden rumbling of the airwaves. And then of course the DesertStorm. And Americana was livid with the ecstasy of the game of war. And NBC and ABC and CNN carried it all for every living moment of death, every sudden boom of hopes exploded into glorious fragments against a weary sky. And then of course the total blankout on our Liberian Civil War.

So Akofa came back home from school with a Social Studies prep: telephone numbers of Congressmen and Senators; she could call and give them her opinion on whether the world should go to war against Saddam Hussein. And somewhere in her twelve-year-old mind, she figured it couldnt be right. "I dont want to talk about their war," she protests. "After all, they dont care about Liberia?" But that is the point, my little woman. People should fight their own wars, count their own losses, and celebrate their own victories, if indeed we still can talk of the victory of war, any war. And yet, how am I to explain that the Gulf Crisis is *Our* Crisis? Back home in structurally adjusted Ghana, the price of fuel jumps from four hundred cedis to one thousand cedis per gallon. Overnight. All because somebody in Wall Street *speculated* that the war could last for years, or may be the Gulf would dry up from excessive nuclear heat. And then of course the Dow Jones Industrial Average could take a suicidal plunge. Fairly simple arithmetic of life.

And about Liberia, Akofa: It would of course be nice, really nice, if the U.S. of A. could care. Especially since as you remember from the history book, after the Americana Dream had used up some of our people and didnt need them anymore, she gathered a whole lot of them and sent them all to Liberia. But you see, we have a real problem here, and we must sympathise with the Americana position. The Liberian War is an Africana problem and then of course it is a *civil* war. This means that for no reason at all, people of the same family decide that they must destroy themselves by killing one another. And they would do it with or without help from anyone. And then of course the United Nations would not permit anyone, not even the United States, to interfere in a family quarrel. The Gulf War was clearly different: The United Nations said anyone who wanted to give exercise to his soldiers could send them to fight Saddam Hussein, because Saddam's war was the Mother of All Wars. And we survived the screaming hysteria of war fever. Now it's time for the victory parade. And as the yellow ribbons of War Joys float along the avenues must I remind myself of how somewhere there may be many fellow humans who even now must wear the blood red banderas of mass slaughter?

And as I pack up my dreams and head back home to Africa, I must keep firm hold on the memories that bring meaning and substance to my brief sojourn here at Cornell where the Africana Center is separated from the main campus with its centers of knowledge and power by a water fall and a deep gorge linked by a narrow bridge closed to traffic for half my stay. I remember Daisy Rowe and her daily hopes for a son sent into the DesertStorm. I remember Carolyn Wells and her sorrow poem for Winnie Mandela on her way to those caves of hate that kept her Nelson in for a generation of nameless pain. I remember Sheila Towner and her silent hope for a more efficient environment for work and play and rest. I remember Anne Adams and how she made time to care for everyone but herself. And Abdul Nanji, the Mwalimu who makes Kiswahili an alternative official language for the business we must conduct for Africana Studies. *Nenda salama, rafiki yangu.*

I must recall the many other scholars who came as visitors

and moved on before we could find the time to compare notes. Among them, Pathe Diagne, one whose whisper is the lion's roar; he who set the house aflame with the broken energy of Bakari II, the mystery Mansa of Ancient Mali who with his 10,000 men and 2000 boats sailed the secret corridors of the turbulent Atlantic and disappeared into South America in 1312 A.D., generations before the birth of Christoph Colomb. Somebody forgot to tell us why poor Colomb just had to go first to West Africa before sailing off into his dream.

I go back home to Africa with one regret: With each one of us caught so deep in our private resistance, there was hardly time for a sustained intellectual fellowship, the deep probing and frank sharing of dreams and doubts beyond our eternal good intentions. Next time for sure, but then Time runs into Eternity even as we get stuck at deadends, even as we pause and hope and fling our anger at the winds. The gorge that separates Africana from Cornell cannot be dammed with corpses of our rage, but with the expanded vision of our mission. When our students—inheritors of our dream—speak with pride about the mystic glories of Ancient Egypt, we must confront them with the reality of Modern Africa. We cannot celebrate vanished civilizations as though between the birth and the death of light those who peopled our dream did not count for much. Yesterday I took Akofa to the Corning Museum of Glass. The exhibits, of course begin with Ancient Egypt. But the official museum history claims the first glass vessels were made in Mesopotamia. The archaeological evidence of Mesopotamia's pride of place can only be excavated from the mythic imagination of the official historian of this magnificent museum of false images and transparent distortions of reality forever fractured in the sharp angle of creative truth.

We cannot assume that truth speaks for itself. Despite Cheikh Anta Diop. Despite Dr. Ben Jochannan, we have had to wait for *Black Athena* for the issue to appear on the official agenda of the academy. And even then, Martin Bernal is still debating footnotes with his learned colleagues. Femi Taiwo, my companion for this season of soulsearch, is still looking for someone who could relieve him of his brains. For a philosophy teacher in a world that would not associate thought with Africa, he certainly has a problem. But Femi, I'm afraid you are stuck with your brains. And you will need it to survive the onslaught of the new mythology of supermen at the brink of new galaxies. Despite the concrete archeological evidence of our claim to the world's premiere civilizations, we still must sort out for ourselves, how we lost our own truth and must live by the alien lies we now believe with the reckless passion of teenage love. That is why the Brother-Sister Communion is hardly enough, unless it means holding hands and together digging deep even into the mess we swim through on our way to everywhere but our desired destination.

Some have tried to negotiate their way around the sadness we call our Blues. Others have tried believing it wasnt there at all. Still others will swear it aint the way is supposed to be and so they couldnt care a tiny bit. But still the Blues remains. And grows so deep it sometimes tastes like indigo and infrared, burning paths of solitude into our carnivals of hope.

June 18, 1991
The Africana Studies &
Research Center,
Cornell University.

PART ONE:

......CaribbeanBlues.....

The Taino in 1992
for Manuel Vargas   for Wilson Harris

Ao! Amigo   Los Amigos

Adios   Domingo
Adios   Santo Domingo

Hispaniola   Hispaniola   Hispaniola
Lost Land of the Taino

Christoph Colomb   Christoph Colomb
Duarte   Sancehz   Mella
Imperial Statues in a Sea of Blood.

The turbulent memory of the Taino
And a hurricane of Arawak sounds.

So they wiped them out
Drowned their screams
Burned their nerves and bones
And scattered their ashes
Across the intimidating splendour
Of this young history of lies.

StormTime in these CaribSeas.

Soon the Hurricanes   the Hurricanes
Shall spring loose
From places of ancient ambush.

They will gather once more
The ancestral anger
Of this land of hostile winds.

In the dying howl
Of Hurricane Columbus
We yet may hear once more
The rising growl
Of the Taino Chieftain
Who opted out of Christ's Kingdom
Where they insist the butcher dog
May come to sup with ArchAngel and God.

Through the infinity of centuries
Forever lost to trauma and to amnesia

We ford ancient oceans of blood
In that final backward glance

Into old chambers
Jammed with presious stones

And firstfruits gathered in savage
Haste from fields nurtured with love
By those careful gaurdians of the Earth:

*"We do not inherit the Earth
from our ancestors ;
We borrow it from our Children".* ← talk about that

Christoph Colomb   Christoph Colomb

Hispaniola   Hispaniola   Hispaniola

Adios   Domingo
Adios   Santo Domingo.

San Pedro de Macoris
for Marino

In these CaneFields
Nourished by silent
Groans of Haitian Immigrants

The Memory caves
in upon History's sad Logic:

Disinherited by Haiti
Repudiated by Republica Dominicana
They shuffle through Life
In the uncertain Dance of the Zombi.

These are the children
of Macandal and Toussaint
of Dessaline and Olivoro Mateo.

But ancestral trophies
Are no valid collateral
For the new industrial enterprise.

Across infinite sadness
Of plantations
Of sorrow grown to harvest point

We intrude upon secrets
As ancient and modern
As inconsolable hurts
In armpits of our Joys.

On the *Batey* you must explain
Abel Williams:
Head of household at 18.
Has never known a girl.
May never know woman.
And he is Head of a family of 8.
Proud inheritor of a father
Who poured out his life
Upon the SugarFields.

And I search for answers still.

And dear Marino   do not
Wonder why I could not
Drink the coffee you made
With so much love and care
As we paused for breath in your home:

I could not take
The cafe-au-Lait.
I could not take it Black.
But above all
I could not take BitterSugar.

The Haitian *Batey*
Is a LivingWound
In the throat of the SugarMill.

Republica Dominicana
for Caryl Phillips

i. Dispossession
It's not the questions you shoot   Caryl
But
The answers you dare undress   Brother.

Not the anger in your hope   Rudy
But
The relentless AncestralLogic

that moves us on and on
through rage to *Higher Ground.*

    with so much waiting to be done
    with so much left so long undone
       to call our situation a dilemma
       is a bad excuse for inaction

Here in the Republica Dominicana
Santo Domingo pursues your primal dreams
across fevers into nightmares
where death lays ambush for your Soul.

The census office undresses your skin
peels your veins
and dilutes your blood.

Dispossessed of your ancestry
your BlackNess
Dissolves into vague regions
of the Indios Myth.

ii. Fiesta Palos

On the fiesta grounds
AncestralLogic reclaims
lost dimensions of the Soul.

Each face   a mask
of agony overwhelmed
by joy of life hatched
in rituals of re-
Birth
in StormFields of Cane Sugar &
Death.

At a command of Drums
the memory door bursts
open to sounds of the countless Dead.
Vibrations grow into tremours into rumblings.
The body quakes and ruptures
into ecstacy of Souls.

The fiesta crowd
surges   and breaks   sways.
The OldMan at its head—
his face a mask of ancestral hurt—
sets the night ablaze with ShootingStars.
The crowd explodes and pours
into the Church
and drives the Angels out.

Outside the Church
a group performs the ResurrectionDance.
The Drums reconstruct foundations of lost HomeLands.
The voice of the BaKongo
rise deep into a sky silenced
by its own lack of creative Truth.

An OldMan—
in another life priest of agrieved dieties—
masters his rage
and leads the dance into a trance
and on and on
into endless transformations of AncestralPain
into constant permutations of Life & Death
of Death & Life in the still centre of RagingStorms.

iii. Tarantula

In the dark
a Tarantula crawls
into my daydream:

   Black.   Hairy.   Contorted.

Full of dis-
crepances and dis-
jointed limbs.

Pitiless and venomous
image
of history's dis-
tortions
of our furious Race.

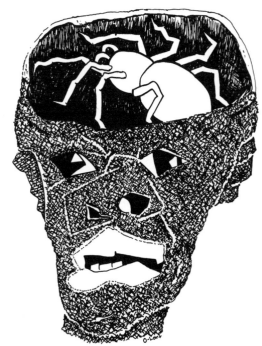

DomingoBlues

Along the Malecon
The splendour halls
Rise arrogantly
Into a sky puzzled
and muzzled by heavy
Burdens of distorted innocence.

And tribesmen of the tourist class—
inheritors of stolen feasts—
Pour out their lives
Into glassed casinos &
Into marbled whorehouses.

The sewers choke and ooze
With rot and rancid breath
Flushing shit and pious fart
Unto the infinite embrace
Of Atlantic's turbulent waves.

Renewal Time

In the nerve centre
of these memory fields

A Taino ancestor bursts
Through Earth and Blood
Plants his Hope into Towers
Above retreating usurper gods.

    Tall.   Proud.
    Naked.   Erect.

Like a Divine Phallus
Ready to explode
Countless ManSeeds
Into WomanEarth for the coming FertileTime.

HavanaSoul

for Armando Entralgo
for Claritta Pulido

So I made the ultimate connection
between two lifetimes set apart
by a final death of old mythologies.

And Havana was still alive
and proud and healthy like a rainbow trout
Forever determined to survive
the sudden death of old comrades.

Across Havana Bay
Along the Malecon
Down the MarinaHemingway

I stand breathless with yearning for strange desires
as the fading sun
sets my memory ablaze with sparks and fireflies.

At the Marina Hemingway I stood among
strange shadows of the imagination and heard
once more the distant call of the inner life of things.
Old Ernest in his greatness looked upon
the calm before the hurrricanes, and planted
his OldMan's dreams where the Ocean Perch
and the Blue Shark may never come to feed.

And Santiago de Cuba haunts me into dawn and dream:

Daisy Castillo with the faraway look in her eyes
speaking soft and deep of how her mother
welcomed Marcus Garvey to Havana of the stormy years.
Her mother—still alive with a mind as sharp as a laser
beam—had
seen this little finger of Earth stuck out in troubled Seas, had
seen this Cuba's run for life survive Baptista's birth & death,
had
seen her island solitude rise to new glory in the east-west trail
Antonio Maceo once carved along the mountain slopes.

And this indeed is Cuba of the fabled Bay of Pigs?

The Royal Palm
Standing still among her Island Solitude:

Tall.   Proud.   Erect
against the storm.
Full of erotic energy.
And yet overwhelmed
by ecstasy of victories
won in a sea of hurricanes.
Lying low & deep in the armpit of the Buffalo Bull.

Now that you've lost all friends
to freedom cyclones of our time
For how long may you survive
the inspiring hate of enemies?
For how long must all your goals
be measured between angles set by devoted opponents?
Suppose the inevitable logic of history

rolls in upon the next hurricane
and deprives you of your dearest enemy,
would you still be firm and steady and royal like the palm?
or will you loosen your hold on the prime purpose for which
Jose Marti and Antonio Maceo and Che Guevara
and all the endless line of valiant ancestors
fought against their doubts and died their own deaths
so that life may be deprived of its eternal hesitations?

I go back now to the baby joys I left
back home in the care of little folk with giant
dreams who bet their children's last hope
against the boasts of tyrant kings.

No one flies the Middle Passage no more.
And for lack of friends along the way
CubanaAir must take me first to Gander of the intemperate
    North.
Then South to Madrid of the arid lands. And AirFrance into
    Paris.
And SwissAir into Zurich. And on and on
to the GoldCoast via the IvoryCoast,
those sometime treasure lands where now
we must embrace the orphan life in small measures of foreign
    aid.

And all our journeys must always take us
away from destinations into disLocations
until one day, tired at last from endless
trailings of lost purpose and lost vision
we mark the only straight route from Ghana to Havana to
    Guyana

and and on and on to Savannah in Georgia of the deep deep
   South.
With AfricanaAirways, we can renavigate the Middle Passage,
   clear
the old debris and freshen the waters with iodine and soul-
   clorine.

And our journey into SoulTime
will be
The distance between the Eye and the Ear.

PAUSE:

... EarthChild...

EarthChild

And still we stand so tall   among the cannonades
We smell of mists and of powdered memories.....

Born to Earth   and   of the Earth
we grew like infant corn among the Locust Clan
we gathered our dawn in armfuls of dust
we blew brainstorms in the night of our birth.

Termintes came and ate away our Voice
ate away our rainbow's gown of flames
soiled memories with wild banquets of blood.

And still we stand so tall   among the fields of thorn
We smell of mists and of scented memories....

There once were gods who came at dawn
and took away our Voice
leaving here the howls of storm
the screams of devotees
the rancid breaths of priest.

But still we stand so tall   among the cannonades
We smell of mists and of powdered memories....

EarthChild   EarthChild   EarthChild
SeyamSinaj   SinajSeyam   SeyamSinaj
EarthChild   EarthChild   EarthChild

your Songs traverse this land of hostile winds
you blow brainstorms into banquet halls of MoonChildren
you die   you live   in Song
you hate   you love   in Song
you measure our joy in interplay of polyrhythmic Sounds.

SinajSeyam   SeyamSinaj   SinajSeyam
EarthChild   EarthChild   EarthChild
SinajSeyam   SeyamSinaj   SinajSeyam

I am   you are   my Song   our dream   my love
our Hope
You sought my Soul   I sought your Soul   so long
in cross rhythms of Jazz   in polyrhythmic miles of Jazz
till Miles   our Davis   led us through the rumbling weight of
Drums
I found   I lost you again   to wails of Saxophones
lost   found you again   in booming hopes of God's
Trombones.

   And still we stand so tall   among the cannonades
   We smell of mists and of powdered memories.....

But come next fall   EarthChild   EarthChild   EarthChild
I may lose you again to pampered dreams of mythmakers
lose you again to imperial dreams of history's pawnbrokers

and all I have is

    a Song for you
    a Song for you
    a Song for you........

You will walk away with all our history braided on you head
all woven into cross rhythms of hair   each strand
so linked to every other strand   each path
so linked to every other path   each destiny
the destiny of evey other   single destiny.

And in all alleyways of   old London   and Paris   and
Lisbon
And in all harlemways of   New York   Chicago   New
Orleans
in Kingston-Jamaica   Havana in Cuba   Atlanta in
Georgia
on Voudoun shores of Haiti   our Haiti   Oh Haiti!
on Voudoun shores of Haiti   Oh Haiti   our Haiti!
on Voudoun shores of Haiti   our Haiti   Oh Haiti!
you will find footprints running backways
into lives once lost to sharp rhythms of Panther's greed
lives all lost   to cold embrace of Atlantic's waves.

SeyamSinaj   SinajSeyam   SeyamSinaj
EarthChild   EarthChild   EarthChild
SinajSeyam   SeyamSinaj   SinajSeyam

I am   you are   my Song   our dream   your dawn
our Love
I sought your Soul   you sought my Soul   so long
in cross rhythms of Jazz   in polyrhythmic miles of Jazz
till Miles   our Davis   took us through the agonies of Joys
and Donny Hathaway checking out   so soon   so young
so good
walking off with all his stuff   with almost all our Song.

I lost   I found you again   in wails of Saxophones
found   lost you again   to rumbling weight of Drums
lost   found you again   in hopeful Booms of God's
Trombones
your voice so strained against the pains the ecstacies.

And still we stand so tall   among the Locust Clan
We smell of mists and of scented memories.....

and yet such menace in casual glance of friends
so much fear in eyes of mythmakers.
Some swear there will be mountains washed away to sea
seagulls flying through our whispered dreams
pains so deep in granite walls of Souls
corncobs left half-burnt from blazes in our mind.

But those who took away our Voice
Are now surprised
They couldn't take away our Song.

EarthChild   EarthChild   EarthChild
SeyamSinaj   SinajSeyam   SeyamSinaj
EarthChild   EarthChild   EarthChild

I Sing I Sing I Sing
A Song   A Hope   A Love

a Song for you
a Song for you
a Song for you......

And still we stand so tall   among the cannonades
We smell of mists and of powdered memories......

And those who took away our Voice
Are now surprised
They couldn't take away our Song.

PART TWO

...AncestralLogic...

Lolita Jones *
for Dzifa   for Maya

And so they says ma Name is Lolita Jones?

But that aint ma real Name.
I never has known ma Name   our Name

I cud'a been Naita   Norwetu
Or may be Maimouna   Mkabayi
Asantewaa   may be Aminata   Malaika.

Ma Name cud'a been sculptured
Into colors of the Rainbow
Across the bosom of our Earth.

But you see:
Long ago   your People sold ma People.
Ma People sold to Atlantic's Storms.

The Storms   first it took away our Voice
Then it took away our Name
And it stripped us of our Soul.

Since then   we've been pulled   pushed
    kicked   tossed   squeezed   pinched
    knocked over   stepped upon   and spat upon.
We've been all over the place
And yet
We aint got nowhere at all.

That's why when the Black Star rose
I flew over to find ma Space

And aint nobody like this Brother
Who gave me back ma Soul.

But you   you kicked hem out
              you pushed him off
              you segregated him from his SoilSoul.

And yet since that fucking day
You all aint done nothing worth a dime!

Now his Soul is gone on home
You sit out here   you mess your head
You drink palm wine   you talk some shit
Just shuckin' n jivin' n soundin'
All signifyin' Nothin'!
You all just arguin' funerals.

Aint nothing gone down here at all
And you all is nothing worth ma pain.

I'll gather ma tears around ma wounds
I'll fly me off to ma QueenDom Come.

I've got me a date with our SoulBrother
And this aint no place for our Carnival.

Just hang out here
   And grind your teeth
   And cry some mess
   And talk some bull
   And drive some corpse to his KingDom Gone.

Why dont you talk of Life for a change?
You all is so hang up with the Dead
And I aint got no time to die just now.

I cudnt care to wait for judgment of your Gods.
There never was no case against our SoulBrother.

It's you all is trial here
But I cudnt care to wait
And hang you even by the Toe.

   You didnt even invite me here at all.
   But I came   &   I spoke ma Soul

---

* The occasion is that of the death in exile of Kwame Nkrumah, the deposed
first President of Ghana. There is an imaginary trial going on in Ghana to
decide whether he deserves to be brought back home for a hero's burial.
Lolita Jones is the final and uninvited witness, testifying to Nkrumah's Pan
African legacy. See "In the High Court of Cosmic Justice", in my earlier collection *Earthchild* (Accra: Woeli Publishing Services, 1985).

For Zora

Sing us a Joy   they plead.

But I sing your Sorrow still.

Like Zora on her lonely quest
for the spirit that keeps
our people standing tall in Storms

I've been in Sorrow's cooking place
licking clean the pots and pans and floors
getting high on sad delight

celebrating Life in spite and because of Death.

Nostalgia

Above all   I shall forever
lament the wisdom
of those many many

Friends who disinherited their Souls
And chose the misery of alien Joys.

   trapped in circles among SnowFields
   their spirits freeze   and thaw   and Frost
   with constant fickleness of NorthernWinds.

Once too often
they converge in smokey PartyRooms
drinking hard   to prove
a point only they   can see   can feel
arguing endless justifications
for a choice sadly made.

Between their dreams of Fame
Their hopes of instant Wealth

the nostalgic self moans its way
through MidNight Storms
into DawnNightmares

   reaching into   distances   silences...

Memories alone are not enough SoulGuide
Into Futures filled with many Absences.

Children of the Land
A Sequence for African Liberation. *
(Version One)

i:

WE are the Children of the Northern Lands.

Our hopes have known the fury of sands and storms.
But like the rolling Saharas of our history
Our dreams have flourished among the oases.

From the mountain peak of Toubkal of the Atlas
We shout our joy across the space of sands

   all the way to Tahat in Ahaggar
   all the way to Tousside in Tibesti

From the Atlantic Coast to the Red Sea
From the ancient Straight of Gibraltar

along the seaboard of the Mediterranean
all the way to Alexandria of our Past and our Future

From the Northern Lands
We come to you with all the wishes of our People.

And if you wish to know us by our Names:

from Nouakchott	I am Mauritania.
from El Aiun	I am Saharui Arab Democratic Republic.
from Rabat	I am Morocco.
from Tunis	I am Tunisia.

from Tripoli   I am Lybia.
and all the way from Cairo of the Pharaohs
                     I am Egypt.

WE are the Children of the Northern Lands.

ii:

WE are the Children of the Eastern Lands.
the lands of the Rising Sun.

Once so long   our hopes were ambushed
        by the Children of the Panther.
But by the fighting skills of our warriors
        we broke the Panther's jaw and pride.

Today   we fold our dreams gently in our arms.

Like the Rift Valleys of our ancient lands
Our roots cut deep into the bosom of our Earth.

With the splendour of Zebra and of the Gazelle
With the miracle and the majesty of the Giraffe
We measure our height against the ancient pride
Of mountains: the Karisimbi   the Ruwenzori   the
    Kilimanjaro.

Our land's beauty is larger than the dream of praise singers.

Our hopes rise deep from the bosom of our Earth
And touch the very forehead of the Sky.

From the mountain glories of our Eastern Lands
We come to you with the victories the worries of our People.

WE are the Children of the Eastern Lands:

```
from Khartoum      I am Sudan
from Addis Ababa   I am Ethiopia of Ancient Fame.
from Djibouti      I am Djibouti
from Mogadishu     I am Somalia
from Kampala       I am Uganda
from Nairobi       I am Kenya
from Kigali        I am Rwanda
from Bujumbura     I am Burundi
from Dar es Salam  I am Tanzania
from LiLongwe      I am Malawi
from Victoria      I am Seychelles Islands
from Moroni        I am Comoro Islands
```

WE are the Children of the Eastern Lands.

iii:

WE are the Children of the Western Lands.
   the lands of the Falling Sun.

Once so long   the Children of the Polar Bear
   set upon our Dream and tore it into shreds.

But by the cunning of our warriors of our Elders
   by the Divine intervention of the Mosquito
Today our hopes rise higher than the Eagles's pride.

We who once did all the farming and the cooking
We'll watch Bear Children feast themselves to Death.

Today we know the taste of Freedom's many joys and pains.

From the Fouta Djalon to the Adamawa
We spread out our hopes into colours of the Rainbow.

Along the Gambia and the Volta and the Niger
We channel our anger into living waters of our harvest Joys.

We've known many seasons before the killer drought:
   the abundance of ancient Ghana and of Mali and of
Songhai.
In our future we dream again the rising harvest Moon.

From ancient mysteries of the Western Lands
We greet you today with the secret wisdom of our People.

WE are the Children of the Western Lands:

from Prair	I am Cape Verde
from Dakar	I am Senegal
from Banjul	I am Gambia
from Bissau	I am Guinea Bissau
from Conakry	I am Guinea
from Freetown	I am Sierra Leone
from Bamako	I am Mali
from Monrovia	I am Liberia
from Ouagadougou	I am Burkina Faso
from Niamey	I am Niger
from Ndjamena	I am Chad
from Abidjan	I am La Cote d'Ivoire
from Accra	I am Ghana
from Lome	I am Togo
from Porto Novo	I am Benin
from Lagos	I am Nigeria

WE are the Children of the Western Lands.

iv:

WE are the children of the Central Lands.

We who once wept in the Valleys
    of the Kasai and the Sangha
Today   our hopes rise higher
    than flood waters of the Kongo.

There once were those who thought
    we would die the shameful death of lepers.
Today   we carry our life
    in the bright flames of our eyes.

Our hopes have stumbled
    down the great boulders of Stanley Falls
But still   we flow on through to Lualaba
    and to our various lakes of Rest of Peace.

The Children of the Earth
must live to taste the many joys of Earth.

From the very heart of Africa
We come to you with all hopes of this Earth our Earth.

WE are the Children of the Central Lands:

from Libreville	I am Gabon
from Brazzaville	I am Congo
from Kinshasa	I am Zaire
from Bangui	I am Central African Republic
from Yaounde	I am Cameroun
from Malabo	I am Equitorial Guinea
from Sao Tome	I am Sao Tome and Principe.

WE are the Children of the Central Lands.

v:

WE are the Children of the Southern Lands.

We have seen much better times of our Earth.
Once more in Time we shall inherit the Peace of our Earth.
We who now moan in the night of Gold Diggers.

Where was it heard before
    that Shaka's Children burn in flames
    and die in holes dug into his Earth?
But that's how it's been with us.

By the miracle of our own minds and hands
We shall carve away the Tiger's claws.

We did it once to the Panther and the Lion and the Bear.
We'll do it and do it once more to the Tiger and his Greed.

From Cabinda round the Cape of Storms and up to Cape
Delgado
We'll once more sleep and dream and work in Peace.

Those who now taste the honey of Freedom's bread
They've known also the blood of Death
    we down South still carry in our voice.

   Namibia shall be FREE!!   *Azania shall be FREE!!!*

From the Southern Lands of Life-Through-Death
We bring to you our people's Fears and Hopes.

WE are the Children of the Southern Lands:

```
from Luanda          I am Angola
from Lusaka          I am Zambia
from Harare          I am Zimbabwe
from Maputo          I am Mozambique
from Gaborone        I am Land of the Tswana
from Mbabane         I am Land of the Swazi
from Maseru          I am Land of the Sotho
from Port Louis      I am Mauritius
from Antananarivo    I am Madagascar.
```

WE are the Children of the Southern Lands
and
WE ALL are the Children of AFRICA!!!

---

* Originally composed at the request of the Ghana National Commision on
Children, for a Flag-Raising Ceremony at the O.A.U. Monument, Accra. The
performance involved selected children from some schools in Accra, July 1984.
See a discussion of the dramatization of this first version of the poem in my
essay "Poetry as Dramatic Performance: The Ghana Experience." *Research in
African Literatures* 22.2 (Summer 1991).

Children of the Land
A Sequence for African Liberation.
(Version Two)

i:

WE are the Children of the Northern Lands.

Our hopes have known the fury of sands and storms.
But like the rolling Saharas of our history
Our dreams have flourished among the oases.

From the mountain peak of Toubkal of the Atlas
We shout our joy across the space of sands

    all the way to Tahat in Ahaggar
    all the way to Tousside in Tibesti

From the Atlantic Coast to the Red Sea
From the ancient Straight of Gibraltar

    along the seaboard of the Mediterranean
    all the way to Alexandria of our Past and our Future

From the Northern Lands
We come to you with all the wishes of our People.

WE are the Children of the Northern Lands.

ii:

WE are the Children of the Eastern Lands.
    the lands of the Rising Sun.

Once so long our hopes were ambushed
    by the Children of the Panther.
But by the fighting skills of our warriors
    we broke the Panther's jaw and pride.

Today we fold our dreams gently in our arms.

Like the Rift Valleys of our ancient lands
Our roots cut deep into the bosom of our Earth.

With the splendour of Zebra and of the Gazelle
With the miracle and the majesty of the Giraffe
We measure our height against the ancient pride
Of mountains: the Karisimbi   the Ruwenzori   the
    Kilimanjaro.

Our land's beauty is larger than the dream of praise singers.

Our hopes rise deep from the bosom of our Earth
And touch the very forehead of the Sky.

From the mountain glories of our Eastern Lands
We come to you with the victories the worries of our People:

WE are the Children of the Eastern Lands:

iii:

WE are the Children of the Western Lands.
   the lands of the Falling Sun.

Once so long   the Children of the Polar Bear
   set upon our Dream and tore it into shreds.

But by the cunning of our warriors of our Elders
   by the Divine intervention of the Mosquito
Today   our hopes rise higher than the Eagles's pride.

We who once did all the farming and the cooking
We'll watch Bear Children feast themselves to Death.

Today   we know the taste of Freedom's many joys and pains.

From the Fouta Djalon to the Adamawa
We spread out our hopes into colours of the Rainbow.

Along the Gambia   and the Volta   and the Niger
We channel our anger into living waters of our harvest Joys.

We've known many seasons before the killer drought:
   the abundance of ancient Ghana and of Mali and of
   Songhai.
In our future   we dream again the rising harvest Moon.

From ancient mysteries of the Western Lands
We greet you today with the secret wisdom of our People:

WE are the Children of the Western Lands:

iv:

WE are the children of the Central Lands.

We who once wept in the Valleys
    of the Kasai and the Sangha
Today   our hopes rise higher
    than flood waters of the Kongo.

There once were those who thought
    we would die the shameful death of lepers.
Today   we carry our life
    in the bright flames of our eyes.

Our hopes have stumbled
    down the great boulders of Stanley Falls
But still   we flow on through to Lualaba
    and to our various lakes of Rest of Peace.

The Children of the Earth
must live to taste the many joys of Earth.

From the very heart of Africa
We come to you with all hopes of this Earth our Earth.

WE are the Children of the Central Lands:

v:

WE are the Children of the Southern Lands.

We have seen much better times of our Earth.
Once more in Time we shall inherit the Peace of our Earth.
We who now moan in the night of Gold Diggers.

Where was it heard before
    that Shaka's Children burn in flames
    and die in holes dug into his Earth?
But that's how it's been with us.

By the miracle of our own minds and hands
We shall carve away the Tiger's claws.

We did it once to the Panther and the Lion and the Bear.
We'll do it and do it once more to the Tiger and his Greed.

From Cabinda round the Cape of Storms and up to Cape
Delgado
We'll once more sleep and dream and work in Peace.

Those who now taste the honey of Freedom's bread
They've known also the blood of Death
    we down South still carry in our voice.

   Namibia shall be FREE!!   Azania shall be FREE!!!

From the Southern Lands of Life-Through-Death
We bring to you our people's Fears and Hopes:

WE are the Children of the Southern Lands
and
WE ALL are the Children of AFRICA!!!

Air ZimBabwe: En Route Victoria Falls.
(for Chris Hesse   for Samora Machel)

ZamBia   ZamBezi   ZimBabwe

ZimBabwe   ZamBezi   ZimZambia

History is but the Future
We should have known in the Past

    So one of these days
    Old Victoria shall have
    to gather her wayward children home.

    If only she knew.   If only.

ZimBabwe   ZamBezi   ZimZambia

    The mysteries of these lands
    Are deeper   loftier than
    The EmpireBuilder's dreams

    And so Victoria flows
    In Majestic Pride
    To the yawning edge of Time:

And Great Victoria
Falls   Tumbling
Down the LivingStones more ancient
Than our vision's fartherest point
More slippery than our sleekest mossy glide.

Mutare   Rusape   Harare
Chirendzi   Chipinge   Chirundu
Chimanimani   Bulawayo   Mbalabala

The Souls of these Names
Are older than the Time
We count across our Mind's spaces.

Mosi oua Tunya!   Mosi oua Tunya!

They are *The Smoke That Thunders!*
Gathering whispers of centuries
Into storms and CannonBlasts!
Mowing Great ZimBabwe down to countless ruins
Bringing silence to The Monomotapa's praise.

If only they knew.   If only.

If only David knew of how
Those Stones outlived
The Monomotapa's Dreams.
If only Cecil knew of how
Those Canyon Roads slashed deep wounds
Across our Earth's belly.

If only they knew.   If only.

History is but the Future
We should have known in the Past.

So one of these days
Poor Victoria shall have
To trek her dream across her own safari of pain
Poor Victoria shall have
To go on back home to her QueenDom Gone.

If only she knew.   If only.

ZimBabwe   ZamBezi   ZimZambia.

If only.   If only she knew.

Victoria-

        FALLS.............!

HarareBlues

To: Herbert Chimhundu
&
for: The Liberators in Search of Liberation.

At the end of the BloodTrail
In aftermath of VictorySongs

we young veterans of armed combat
are left abandoned & stranded
on the outskirts of the new life:

Once   we dropped
            out of school   out of trade   out of life.
We took up guns
            to reclaim the lost ancestral land.
            to rename and reown the land.

With blood flowing freely from our souls
We dammed the tide against the storms.

In deep forests   in desperate caves   and grave trenches
Death roared around our heads our lives our souls

            snatched from our arms lifelong comrades
            tore them apart & threw them back
            at us: dismembered beyond reclaim.

But there was a hope that always kept
Our spirits floating above the carnage

The land we knew and loved with such fearsome hope
Covered our footprints with gentle stirring of the soil.

And then one day at noon they set our night ablaze
with bonfires.   Suspended battle cries.   Composed
An anthem tatooed with hopes & lingering doubts.

One day at noon   peacemakers came
and set our night ablaze with bonfires.
abolished battle songs   and planted
their mulatto constitution in our soul.

Then they marched us back to LowFields
and
To old TownShips still stranded in the Storm.

And the pastured land flows like troubled dreams
into endless mirages along the distant rainbow line.

And we who once roamed the deep forests
And shared our land's secret seeds with bird & beast
Are now huddled into little corners of the nation's life
so utterly stranded among the rotten stench
Of Harare's secret wounds & hidden traps.

In our eyes old flames of hope now smoulder
Into volcanic embers   burnig silent streams
Of venomous gas leakage into the city's ventricles.

With arms forever outsretched into solitude
We drink down our permanent anger
From spectacular calabashes so large
They must contain the overspill of war memories.

Beware   Brother   Beware
Beware the hand that reaches down:

Each tattered bosom hides a knife more
Deadly than the venomous viper's fangs.

Each night in a flash of steel
The blood still flows into old sewers
Irrigating the soil & draining down
Sacrificial lives in hope to appease

The Souls that won the War   But lost the Peace.

PAUSE

...The Song of a Twin Brother...

The Song of a Twin Brother
(To Kofi Awoonor)

Stand unshod upon the terrazzo floors of your balcony
Look over the barricade
to the savanna grasslands of your countryside
Silence the stereo soundz of your radiogram
Open your Soul
to the mellow tones of your country brother's xylophone.

    So many Moons ago,
    Before our world grew old,
    I had a Twin Brother.
    We sucked the same Breast
    Walked the same Earth,
    But dreamt of worlds apart.

And here I am today,

    Holding on to Grandfather's sinking boat
    While Atsu my Twin Brother
    Floats on air in Jumbo Jets
    And stares into the skies
    And dreams of foreign ports.

Atsu e e e!
Atsu e e e!

    Do not forget the back without which there is no front.
    Dada is still alive   but grown silent
    And full of songs sung in a voice
    That hints of a heart overstrained
    With the burdens of a clan without Elders.

    Our roof is now a sieve   Atsu.
    The rains beat us.   Beat us.
    Even in our Dreams.
    And the Gods   they say   are not to blame.

The State Farms have dug the thatch and burnt its roots.
They grow rice.   And cane sugar.

    But Oh! Atsu.
    My Twin Brother   Atsu!
    Our bowels are not made for the tasty things of life.
    The rice   the sugar   all go to Accra
    For people with clean stomachs and silver teeth
    To eat and expand in their borrowed glory.

Atsu e e e!
Astu leeee!!!

I shall give your name to the winds.
They will roam the world for you.

You forget,

Atsu my father's former son
You forget the back without which there is no front.

Papa has lost his war against hernia.
Seven Keta Market Days ago,
We gave him back to the soil.
And Dada is full of Nyayito songs:
sorrowing songs sung in a voice whose echoes
float into the mourning chambers of your soul.

Danyevi leeeee!!!

Dada says
The tasty things of life are good
But
You do not chase Fortune beyond the point
Where Old Sky bends down to have a word with Earth.
You do not bury your arm in Fortune's Hole.

There have been others before   Atsu
There have been others before you.

Armattoe went away
    Came and went again.
    Then he never came.

Katako too went away.
    Came and went again.
    Then he came.   But without his Soul.

Atsu,

    I sit under this Oak where you and I once sat
    and cast cowries in the sand.
    I close my eyes.   I give your name to the winds.
    They will roam the world and find your Ears.

Fofonyevi leeeee!!!

    Papa has gone to Tsiefe.
    Dada is full of Nyayito songs.
    And I   Etse   your Twin Brother
    My heart overflows with unsung durges.

    Many many Moons ago,
    Before the Silence came,
    I had a Twin Brother.

    We shared the same Mat.
    But parted in our Dreams.

PART THREE

.......Santrofi Anoma.......*

---

* *The Artist as Santrofi Anoma* : The Dilemma Bird of Akan Mythology.
Society, as Hunter, carries Santrofi home and brings misfortune home; aban-
dons Santrofi in the wilderness and leaves behind great fortune.

DesertStorm
for Naana & for Obiba

i.
So where does one begin?
On what note must we
strike this long distance call
to those things we should have done
things we should be doing with our lives?

Simply then to say sorry.
sorrow for the long silence
beyond the market-place of iron-birds.
You were flying in
from the land of hostile winds   &
I was flying away into new snowstorms.

And here I am today,
still holding on
to fragments of resolutions
made once so many times
in those heady days of dreams:
The Hope   The Promise   Somehow
no matter how far afield
the HoneyBee may fly
he must swim the FireFloods
back to his MotherHive
where they say the honey
flows in slow driblets,
the QueenBee's labours
forever lost to wayward
dreams of MoonChildren.

ii.
Just returned from Old London.
Yes   I've been to London
I've been to London   not
to look at the Queen   but
bear witness in the troubling case
of Power   Marginality   & Oral
Literature in Africa
held at faraway courts
of Oriental & African Studies.

So I flew into Old London
in that night of the Death/Line
for Saddam   &
for his warrior angels of the apocalypse.
The heavens broke loose next day,
you remember?
and all we do now
is listen   even in our sleep
to the screaming hysteria
of war tales told in the relentless relay
of Uncle Sam's Braggart Boys.

It is the age of Old Generals
all dressed in shiny medals
issuing hourly briefs
from cozy conference rooms.
And out there in the Gulf
A widowed mother's only son
Bleeds to Death in DesertStorms.

And all the President's Men
say it is the greatest thing to do:
To call for war and watch The War
from the safe distance
of a whitehouse fortified
against the raging tide of blood
against the lurking danger of the ArmBush.

iii.
And after glorious Booms
of the StarWars Show
the ruthless logic of war
takes over and drives us all—
inevitably the say—
back into sad old times
where war is not   cannot   be
a game of kids played on video screens
by infantmen   but a meal of death
cooked in blood and served redhot
at flashpoint of gun and smoke
and the choked breath.

And when it is all over
we shall once more inherit
a generation of cracked souls
for whom we must erect new
monuments and compose new
anthems of praise and the eternal hope of life
beyond the recurring stupidity of war heroes.

January 31 1991.

Santrofi

for Jack Mapanje

I.
Santrofi   Santrofi   Santrofi

against persistent rumours
of your midnight
death by stabbing squads
I must compose this suicide note
in stupid solidarity with a foolish friend.

Like you   my mind is burdened
with ancestral indiscretion.
The slightest lie
gives us indigestion
so we must go gathering dangerous rumours
letting our minds loose on laxative
soiling popular images of decent people.

They say it's sad for a full-grown
Man with chilldren who call him
Papa   to stagger home in tears.

But Santrofi   I couldnt help maself.

When I heard they say they say
they picked you up at deaf of night

I could not hold on to my pride.

I broke up in fears   I crumbled
home sobbing through my tears.

II.
But then the children started wailing.

So I laughed.   I laughed I told them
I was rehearsing my part in a difficult play.

So they laughed. The children laughed.
But then they asked to see my script
so they could cheer and prompt me on.

Santrofi   I had to explain
there was no script to our play.

We act it out
by daily dress rehearsals
of the various things we shouldnt do.
The drama unfolds backward
with every step we take forward.
The plot quickens and complicates
with unexpected & twisted
reenactments of scenes from future dreams.
We are hurled into false resolutions
leaving us still entangled in strange
subplots
forever groping for redirection
back into our main
conflict with its knotted
quest for a breath of air free of all toxic substances.
We grow breathless yearning
for escape from suffocating assemblies
of shameless men with their poisonous speech
persuading us all to die once more
and die all over again.

But Santrofi   against
their kind offer
of death by stabbing squads
we must insist on our dream
of life   our dream
of life   our dream
of life among the burning grass
   life among the riding storms
      among the desert sands
of life among the thunderbolts.

III.
Santrofi   Santrofi   Santrofi

you remember how
often I came for you at dawn
our shotguns all loaded and ready
for the ancestral partridge hunt?

We were such great badshots
our bullets run away from our game.

But we always came back home.
We always came back home.
Back home to our meal of modest
corn and fish and life.
We always came back home.

So when your Maimouna
in a voice grown eerie with sudden pain
told of how
some nervous men with tangled beards
came for you & walked you
into the deepness of their night
fiercely clutching stolen rifles

I have been wandering
what BigGame hunters club
you may have joined on secret oath.

I have listened every night and every dawn
for the lonely echo of the hunter's call

But all I hear is this silence
deeper than the liar's yawn.

IV.
Santrofi   Santrofi   Santrofi

so now   I am guilty.   Guilty
of harbouring doubts and fears

doubts for their smiles
fears for your mind
fears for your life
fears fears fears for those joys
we dared to dream for our land.

I suppose they'll come with pincers
probing our tongue for unspoken curses.

And we wish we could hold our breath forever.

But once too often we've held
our doubts and found unspeakable
terror in silence and patience
when marvelous blockheads
took up megaphones and broke
eardrums with philosophical obscenities

and baboons in mufti & native sandals
made menacing speeches from platforms

borne on shoulders of those who chose

patience and silence in spite of doubts
silence and patience in spite of doubts

in spite of bleeding fear
in spite of leaking hurt

silence and patience in spite of doubts
patience and silence in spite of doubts.

Santrofi   Santrofi   Santrofi.

V.
Santrofi   Santrofi   Santrofi

you remember
how once upon our doubts
they planted letters in the press

and in the names of mythical voices
they painted our names with dung and slime?

Santrofi   Santrofi   Santrofi

VI.
Santrofi   Santrofi   Santrofi

Today   the fierce young ones
who broke the dawn with smoking guns
are now become Youthful Elders of State.

How come
    they see so much guilt
    in every elder's eyes?
    and hear so much betrayal
    in every intellectual's sneeze?

They bypassed warnings
and took huge loans
only to import
halfwits from
harvard & princeton
halfwits & gifted inventors
of designer deaths in manmade seasons of drought.

Santrofi   Santrofi   Santrofi

you must lay ambush at hellgate
and watch them trespass into limbo
and lead them stranded and lost
among the ghosts of false prophets.

and do us a favour   will you?
Throw a little red pepper in their eyes.
And do not wipe away their tears.

Angels may come and offer you QueenDoms
But whatever you do
Do not wipe away their tears. Eh! Santrofi!!

Bayonets

BEFORE the season of the Bayonet
   there was the season of the Hoe
   a season of the soul's harvest:
   We grew wonder-eyed standing
   humbled before the miracle
   of the giant Oak locked deep
   down within the tinniest mystery seed.

   In those seasons of our Soul's Harvest
   there were such fires in our eyes.
   Our spirits flowered and petalled
   into hues of faintest rainbows
   offering new and newer images
   of dreams we could with ten fingers
   mould into things and thoughts and hopes.

THEN   they came with BullDozers.
And then   the ArmouredCars   dressed in camouflage.

NOW   we plant grenades in backyard farms
Harvesting Coffins
in showers of Bullets and FirePower.

They pick our flesh on Bayonets.

Across cold muzzles of Guns
They break our sleep in two
Give one half to CannonBlast
Toss one half into silence deeper
Than Volcano's bleeding core.

There will be showers at SunRise
And storms at SunDrown.
Bones shall sprout tendrils more verdant
Than loveliest GreenMamba.

Rivulets of venom shall water our fields
Restoring this soil to ancestral Fertile Time.

Of Dreams & Doors

They shut the doors against our hopes.

They shut   shut   shut the doors
   against our dreams.

   shut   seal   bolt the doors
   against our dreams.

They close the doors against our screams.

They close   close   close the doors
   against our dreams
   against our pleas
   against our dreams   our pleas   our screams
   against   against   against our hopes.

They toss our hopes against the rocks.

They toss   toss   toss our hopes
against the wall   against the wall.
   toss   fling   smash our dreams
   against our fears
   against   against   against the rocks.

They shut   shut   shut the Sun
                  against our Day.

Guilt

i.
And they opened up his wound.
Polished its tender surface
With alligator pepper
And onion paste.

But his soul was large
Enough to hold his hurt.

Grasping tight
To sharp painpoint of breath
He threw them back that final
Look
Whose depths they feared to explore.

A Look suspended
somewhere
Between surprise and wonder
Carefully balanced
Between desire to
Hope
And the need to
Believe
That fear   sometimes
Is a noble retreat from
Doom.

ii.
He swore he would be Human   If
Only they would let him   Be.

But they hanged him all the same.

Except that even in death
They could not look him in the face.

There were such questions
On lips of this corpse
Whose memory survives life survives death.

The LawMakers don themselves
in weeds thick enough
To parry the thorniest Question Mark.

The HangMen gather
Their courage around their fear
Assuring themselves in whispers
Even they themselves cant hear:

   It really was a duty by The Law.

But they hanged him all the same.
And they couldnt look him in the face.
But they hanged him all the same.

The Eagle's Pride

And when our Elders
saw the Vulture
perch upon our Royal Palm
They shook their Beards
in memory of the Eagle's Pride.

Still,
there were those who whispered:

    the season of the Panther
    and
    the season of the Cobra

    must come to pass
    even
    in our very days.

Simply   just quite simply
we'll raise our brows
in memory of
The Vulture's feast of rot.

WE   so young   have seen
The Panther in his sudden

    Leap   of   Death.

We yet may see the King Cobra
And his rain/reign of Poison Kisses.

Redeemers

They came with a Bouquet of CobWebs
Sang obscene songs
Over our sacred images
Their huge nostrils still clogged
With dust and steamy breath.

They were sent to persuade us all
Against our very selves
So we in our delusion
Would deny our own follies
Spending seasons pretending to Divinity.

But our Human flesh stuck to our bones
Like sweat on dirt on goosepimples
Stuck to our bones like dirt on sweat
Till our Souls stood naked and humbled
Before noble passions that moved us still
Even among our many blunders.

We stood among our many broken dreams.
And oh we saw our old follies kneel in low profile
Against the blazing Western Sky.

They came with a Bouquet of CobWebs
Sang obscene songs
Over our sacred images of Self and Gods
Their huge nostrils still clogged
With dust and steamy breath.
In their hands a kind offer of Holy Death.

But our Human flesh stuck to our bones
And noble passions still move us on
Even among our many blunders.

History & Blindness

Once we snatched our heads
from jaws of Polar Bear

And now with our own hands
we offer our hearts for safe-keeping
to the Panther prowling round
the outskirts of our lives
reclining under ancestral communal trees
laying ambush in that midday snooze
in which even dreams
take on the density of fear.

Let us not deceive ourselves
believing the future is
but a photocopy of the past.

If the wisdom of the elders
were proof against disasters

their hopes would not have lost
heirlooms in the noonday
spark that set the sea ablaze.

Old Lizzard

I am Old Lizzard
with my stomach aches
stuck away
under the rhythm of my breath.

I laugh rainbows
through screams into many miles of hurt
through pains that stretch into endless memory.

Only the setting Sun
Can tell what treasures lay
Beyond the mountain clouds.

But Children of ButterFly
now wrap themselves
in borrowed Velvet Robes
Hop the skies and dare the rays
Pretending
They are chosen inheritors
Of our Sun's Glory.

And I who scaled the loftiest dizzy heights
Fallen off the tallest Odum tree
I've peeped over horizon's final curtained Stop.
And
I've seen our Sun retreat
Before the Blanket Anger of the Night.

So I can only nod and nod and nod my Head
In knowing futility of Velvet's dreams.

Let ButterFly Children hope and dream the skies
in borrowed Velvet Robes
pretending
they are chosen inheritors
of our Sun's Glory.

I can only nod and nod and nod my burdened head
I   Old Lizzard   with my stomach aches
Stuck away under the rhythm of my breath.

Novimo

RainDrop in the Sun
She was a Rain-
Drop in our Sun.

In her gentle
Breeze of Voice
She caught all
Splendours of our World.

And in her deep
Ripples of Breath
Our rivers found
Primordial confluence with Stars.

Husago Dance

One day   quite simply
I shall set one brief
Step upon the long
Road into SoulSpace.

With a teasing grin
On my stupid face
I shall take a final
Look at all the things
I should have done.

Somewhere Up on a tiny
Branch of our ancestral tree
I shall perch and watch
The *Husago* Drums
Dance Life out of Death.

A Love Supreme

Beyond   Beauty of the Body
There is Beauty of the Mind.

Beyond   Beauty of the Mind.
There is Beauty of the Person.

Beyond   Beauty of the Person.
There is Beauty of the Soul.

From RestLess Joys of FretFul Love
I trail glories into contours of your Mould.

I trace the Topo-Beauty of your Soul
In the gentle Rise & Fall & Curve of Lips & Hips.

My Passions Rise & Fall & Break
Like surfs upon your many Shores.

Along your spinal stretch of Rift Valleys
I stumble unto
Deep & Secret Joys of Love & Peace.

In your QuickSands of ancient MysteryCaves
I feel Eternity flash across horizons of my Mind
Then   The Bottom Drops out of my Breath!

REST

...Fertility-Game...

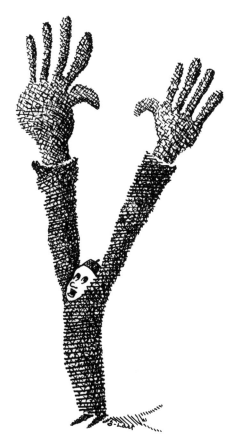

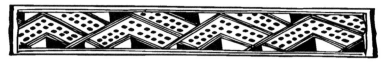

Fertility Game

Come back home   Agbenoxevi   Come back home.

A week today at carnival time
young men of the land will gather
for the wrestling duel of song and dance,
maidens will sharpen their tongues   and
carve praise images of dream lovers   and
I have a gourdful of praise names   laid aside for you.

Come back home   Agbenoxevi   Come back home.

In the eyes of town
I will break the evil glance of witches
I will pour you a calabash of pride
I will hold it firm to your lips
till your eyes catch the gleam of stars
till your mind reaches out for moons
till your body vibrates to rhythms of the seas.

Come back home   Agbenoxevi   Come back home.

And your voice shall rise deep   across the years
through rainbow gates to the beginnings of things.
It will come floating through seasons of glory
thundering through deserts and painfields
where our people died the death of droughts and of wars
where they died   and   lived again
where they die   and   wake up
with seeds of life sprouting from their graves.

Come back home   Agbenoxevi   Come back home.

Agbenoxevi   Atsu Agbenoxevi
I have held my passion in check for you
holding it fast against storms   against thunder
held it firm against the haunting smiles of gods
I have strained my bosom against the sharp edges
of harmattan winds   against the rumbling weight
of May RainStorms.
I am the rainbow standing guard
across your path of Storms.

Atsu   I have died a hundred deaths for you
Each time each night   I wake up again and again
in that house we built upon the shores
with pools of troubled seas.

      Come back home   Agbenoxevi   Come back home.

All   all my peers now carry big babies on their back
Still   I carry mine in my heart.   Sometimes in my loins.
And O she cries so much for you.

      Come back home   Agbenoxevi   Come back home.

Kokui   my young sister   went away last Moon
at harvest time. She swallowed a tiny gourd seed
So now she carries a giant gourd in her belly
for Senyo our dying Chief's only living son
Even Foli   my mother's youngest child
now speaks in the broken voice of a ManChild
They say   at the village school   he goes
pinching all the bigger girls on their wosowosos
They always scream   but   they never report him
And once the teacher caught him
he explained O it was only a little test

to hear the difference in voice pitches
of teenage girls and teenage boys

They say they let him off and now he comes boasting
he's man enough to handle a thousand meddling teachers
He even talks of a swift madness there may be
in these words I give to winds for you.

      Come back home   *Agbenoxevi*   *Come back home.*

I have woven a hundred songs for you   woven them
all into pillows for your wandering head of dreams
For your bed   I plucked feathers from peacock's pride
Each midnight moonlight night   I walk naked
to the crossroads towards the falling place of Sun
I lean against the firm bosom of our ancient baobab tree
I close my eyes   I give your name to west-bound winds

And in a careless abandon to joys there are in songs
I stretch my breast against the Moon's Glory   just
waiting to dance you home to your rainbow bed
where you and I may wrestle again   all over again
in that old Fertility-Game   first played by Gods
in the seedtime of our Earth.

      Come back home   *Agbenoxevi*   *Come back home.*

I say today I stand naked beneath our baobab tree
watching yor dreams running along the path of storms

I will woo you yet with glories of the Moon   while
our hunters break their tongues in strange whispers
of MoonDeity at life's crossroads
keeping vigil for SunGod's homecoming

from ramblings across the skies
through Thunder's gates and Lightning's path
into house of fugitive dreams

Come back home   Agbenoxevi   Come back home.

Come with me to your rainbow bed
where you and I may wrestle again   and again
all over again   in that old Fertility-Game
first played by Gods   in the seedtime of our Earth.

Come back home   Agbenoxevi   Come back home.

The End

About the Author:
Kofi Anyidoho is both a poet and literary scholar, a specialist of African and African-heritage literatures. He teaches at the University of Ghana, Legon. He is also a founding member of the Management Committee of the W.E.B. DuBois Memorial Centre for Pan African Culture, Accra, Ghana. His three previous poetry collections are Elegy for the Revolution (1978), A Harvest of Our Dereams (1984), and Earthchilld (1985).